Mathematics

FOR COMMON ENTRANCE

13+

Exam Practice Answers

David E Hanson

GALORE PARK

AN HACHETTE UK COMPANY

Although every effort has been made to ensure that website addresses are correct at time of going to press, Galore Park cannot be held responsible for the content of any website mentioned in this book. It is sometimes possible to find a relocated web page by typing in the address of the home page for a website in the URL window of your browser.

Hachette UK's policy is to use papers that are natural, renewable and recyclable products and made from wood grown in sustainable forests. The logging and manufacturing processes are expected to conform to the environmental regulations of the country of origin.

Orders: please contact Bookpoint Ltd, 130 Milton Park, Abingdon, Oxon OX14 4SB. Telephone: (44) 01235 827720. Fax: (44) 01235 400454. Email education@bookpoint.co.uk Lines are open from 9 a.m. to 5 p.m., Monday to Saturday, with a 24-hour message answering service. Visit our website at www.galorepark.co.uk for details of other revision guides for Common Entrance, examination papers and Galore Park publications.

ISBN: 978 1 4718 4695 3

© David E Hanson 2015

First published in 2015 by

Galore Park Publishing Ltd,

An Hachette UK Company

Carmelite House

50 Victoria Embankment

London EC4Y 0DZ

www.galorepark.co.uk

Impression number 10 9 8 7 6 5

Year 2019

Some illustrations by Ian Moores were re-used. All other illustrations by Aptara, Inc.

Typeset in India by Aptara, Inc.

Printed in Great Britain by Hobbs the Printers Ltd, Totton, Hampshire.

A catalogue record for this title is available from the British Library.

Contents

Introduction

This book includes all answers for the questions in the *Mathematics FOR COMMON ENTRANCE 13+ Exam Practice Questions* book of the same series.

→ The curriculum and the examination syllabus

The mathematics curriculum and the examination syllabus are subject to relatively minor changes or different emphases from time to time, whereas the body of mathematical skills and knowledge which teachers consider valuable seems to remain fairly constant.

For completeness, and to allow greater flexibility in the use of this material, some questions included in *Mathematics FOR COMMON ENTRANCE 13+ Exam Practice Questions* may be outside the syllabus currently examined, even though they are likely to be within the capability of the majority of students in most schools. It is left to teachers to select questions which they consider appropriate and it is assumed that teachers will wish to differentiate according to student abilities.

The material is appropriate for KS3 studies but, for completeness, questions cover ideas met in all years up to Year 8.

The contents pages outline the way in which questions have been grouped in six 'strands': Number; Calculations; Problem solving; Algebra; Geometry and measures; Statistics and probability. The sections within the strands have been numbered for easier reference.

Examination levels

Level 1 and Level 2 papers are based upon the same syllabus, but *some* of the questions in Level 1 papers will be generally more accessible.

Many of these questions will be accessible to all students and it is assumed that teachers and parents will wish to encourage students to attempt questions that may be just beyond the requirements for the intended examination.

It is expected that the majority of students will take Level 2 papers.

Some extension questions are included for the interest of capable students and are indicated in the text in *Mathematics FOR COMMON ENTRANCE 13+ Exam Practice Questions*.

Questions that are more demanding and *may* be more appropriate for candidates taking papers at Level 2 and above are indicated by a Level 2 symbol in *Mathematics FOR COMMON ENTRANCE 13+ Exam Practice Questions*. Level 3 and CASE papers are based upon the extended syllabus, and questions appropriate for Level 3 and CASE candidates are indicated by a Level 3 symbol in *Exam Practice Questions*. The level indicators are not printed in this *Answers* book.

The level notes are included as a guide only and most of the questions are suitable for students taking papers at any level.

It is strongly recommended that reference is made regularly to the current examination syllabus and to recent past papers.

→ Using Mathematics FOR COMMON ENTRANCE 13+ Exam Practice Questions

The book has been designed for use by students, under the guidance of a teacher or parent, as a resource for practice of basic skills and recall of knowledge.

It is assumed that, in addition to plain paper, the following grids will be available for use where appropriate:

- centimetre squared
- centimetre square dotted

- centimetre isometric dotted

- graph (cm and 2mm).

If students are permitted to draw in the *Exam Practice Questions* book, then valuable time may be saved.

Students are expected to

- show full working where appropriate and, at all times, to make their method clear to the marker

- produce a personal record of achievement which will prove valuable as an additional revision aid.

It is assumed that, throughout, students will

- make use of estimation skills

- pay attention to the order of operations (BIDMAS or BODMAS)

- use strategies to check the reasonableness of results

- use a calculator *only* when instructed or allowed to do so.

Whilst this book has been compiled for use in independent schools, it is expected that it will also prove useful for students in state schools and home schoolers.

→ The questions

Questions follow the ISEB format and are numbered either:

1 (a)   (b)   (c)   where parts of questions are *not* related.

or

1 (i)   (ii)   (iii)   where parts of questions *are* related.

Almost all of the questions are modelled on questions from past Common Entrance 13+ papers, using similar wording and mark allocation.

Within each broad group of questions, some grading in difficulty has been attempted and harder questions may be found towards the end of each grouping. Many of these harder questions will be within the capabilities of most students.

Many questions involve several skills. These questions have been placed wherever seemed most appropriate.

The number of questions on a particular topic reflects the frequency with which such questions have appeared in the Common Entrance papers.

→ Using Mathematics FOR COMMON ENTRANCE 13+ Exam Practice Answers

It is hoped that students will be permitted to write and draw in their copies of *Examination Practice Questions*, since this will save time, especially with graphical work and, also make marking more straightforward.

Teachers and parents will decide on the way that they wish students to present their work for marking.

In questions where stages of working and/or explanations are expected, credit should be given for evidence of appropriate reasoning. Where drawings are involved, it is suggested that evidence of understanding is more important than accuracy.

→ Calculators

Questions in 1.1, 1.2, 2.1 and 2.2 should be tackled *without* a calculator.

In 3.1, 4.2, 5.2 and 6.1 a calculator should not be needed.

Questions in 2.3 *require* the use of a suitable calculator.

Questions which involve both calculator and non-calculator parts have the parts clearly indicated.

It is assumed that students will

● be encouraged to tackle all other questions *without* the use of a calculator.

● have the opportunity to decide for themselves when the use of a calculator is appropriate and when other methods are more effective.

→ Final preparations for the exam

Familiarity with a selection of recent past papers *of the appropriate level* will remind students of what can be expected.

Students at any Level will sit three papers:

● a non-calculator paper of the appropriate Level

● a calculator paper of the appropriate Level

● a mental arithmetic test which is common to all three Levels.

→ Tips on taking the exam

Before the exam students should

● get all their equipment ready the night before. They will need: calculator, pens, pencils, rubber, pencil sharpener, ruler, protractor, compasses, set square.

● make sure they are at their best by getting a good night's sleep before the exam.

● have a good breakfast in the morning.

● take some water into the exam if this is allowed.

● think positively and keep calm.

1 Number

1.1 Properties of numbers

1 (i) 31 or 37 (1) (iii) 36 (1)

  (ii) 35 (1) (iv) 40 (1)

2 (i) 36 (1) (iv) 5 (1)

  (ii) 3 (1) (v) 64 (1)

  (iii) 21 (1)

3 (i) 12, 28 (1) (iv) 1, 9, 25 (2)

  (ii) 1, 2, 5, 15 (1) (v) 1, 27 (2)

  (iii) 2, 5 (2)

4 (a) 14 (2)

  (b) $^-39$ (3)

  (c) 7 and 23, 11 and 19, 13 and 17 (2)

  (d) $2 \times 3 \times 5^2$ (3)

5 (a) $2^4 \times 5 \times 7$ (3) (b) 18 900 (3)

6 (i) $2^3 \times 7$ (2) (ii) 14 (= 2×7) (1)

7 (i) $3^2 \times 5 \times 11$ (3) (ii) 3, 11, 33 (1)

8 (i) 2×3^3 (2) (ii) 6 (1)

9 (i) $2^8 \times 3$ (3) (ii) 3 (1)

10 (i) (a) 2 (1)   (ii) (a) ⁻10 (1)

(b) ⁻3 (1)   (b) 6 (1)

(c) 11 (1)   (c) 16 (1)

(d) 6 (1)   (d) ⁻2 (1)

11 (a) (i) 7 thousand (1)

(ii) 3 hundredths (1)

(b) 0.59, 0.95, 5.09, 5.9, 9.05, 9.5 (3)

(c) 14.32, 14.23, 13.42, 13.24, 12.43, 12.34 (3)

12 (i) 5, 5.055, 5.5, 5.505, 5.55 (3)

(ii) 0.55 (1)

13 6.006, 6.06, $6\frac{1}{3}$, 6.4, 6.51 (3)

14 $\frac{13}{20}$, 66%, $\frac{2}{3}$, 0.67 (3)

15 (a) (i) 3410 (1)   (b) (i) 27.6 (1)

(ii) 200 (1)   (ii) 0.34 (1)

(iii) 59 (1)   (iii) 35.2 (1)

(iv) 0.310 (2)

16 (a) (i) 36 (1)   (b) (i) 60 (1)

(ii) 3 (2)   (ii) 40 (3)

17 (a) 6 (2)

(b) 3000 cm² (3)

18 (a) (i) XXV (1)   (b) (i) 28 (1)

(ii) CVII (1)   (ii) 56 (1)

(iii) MLXVI (1)   (iii) 787 (1)

(iv) MMXV (1)   (iv) 2666 (1)

19 (a) (i) 4.9×10^3 (1)   (b) (i) 1 800 000 (1)

(ii) 7.5×10^{-4} (1)   (ii) 0.003 2 (1)

1.2 Fractions, decimals, percentages; ratio

1 (a) (i) $\frac{3}{7}$ (1)   (b) (i) $\frac{8}{20}$ (1)

(ii) $\frac{1}{4}$ (2)   (ii) 0.4 (1)

(iii) 40% (1)

2 (a) $\frac{5}{8}$ (1)   (c) (i) 3.25 (2)

(b) (i) $3\frac{2}{3}$ (1)   (ii) 35% (2)

(ii) $\frac{9}{2}$ (1)

3 (5)

Fraction	Decimal	Percentage
$\frac{7}{20}$	0.35	35%
$\frac{1}{4}$	0.25	25%
$1\frac{1}{5}$	1.2	120%
$\frac{3}{20}$	0.15	15%

4 (a) $\frac{13}{50}$ (2)   (c) £3.20 (2)

(b) 0.65 (2)

5 (i) (a) 0.45 (2)   (ii) $\frac{2}{5}$ $\frac{4}{9}$ 45% (1)

(b) 0.4 (2)

(c) 0.44 (2)

6 (a) 0.63 (2)   (c) $\frac{9}{50}$ (2)

(b) 35% (2)   (d) £20.80 (2)

7 (a) £30.40 (2)

(b) (i) $\frac{4}{5}$ (2)

(ii) £360 (2)

(c) 3.02 m (2)

8 (a) £132   (3)   (b) 23%   (3)

9 (a) $\frac{12}{25}$ (2)   (c) £7.50   (2)

   (b) 0.28   (2)   (d) 22 grapes   (2)

10 (i) £6.40   (iii) £1.60

   (ii) £3.20   (iv) £11.20

   The total cost including VAT is £75.20   (4)

11 (a) (i) £16.50   (2)   (b) (i) £112   (1)

          (ii) £46.50   (1)   (ii) 40%   (2)

12 (a) (i) $\frac{3}{20}$ (3)

          (ii) 40 tins   (2)

   (b) 15 days   (2)

13 (a) 9   (2)   (c) 20 tins   (2)

   (b) $\frac{5}{12}$ (2)

14 (a) $\frac{3}{5}$ (1)

   (b) $\frac{4}{5}$ shaded   (1)

   (c) (i) $1\frac{1}{12}$ (2)

       (ii) $\frac{5}{12}$ (2)

15 (a) $\frac{1}{4}$ (2)   (c) $2\frac{1}{12}$ (2)

   (b) $\frac{4}{9}$ (2)   (d) $1\frac{8}{15}$ (3)

16 (a) $\frac{11}{12}$ (2)   (c) $6\frac{1}{12}$ (2)

   (b) $8\frac{1}{4}$ (2)   (d) $\frac{11}{12}$ (3)

17 (a) $4\frac{4}{15}$ (3)   (c) $2\frac{1}{16}$ (3)

(b) $9\frac{1}{2}$ (3)   (d) $2\frac{54}{77}$ (3)

18 £21 (2)

19 (i) £138 000 (2)

(ii) £139 000 (2)

(iii) 7.1% (2)

20 (i) (a) 0.5714 (1)

(b) 0.5333 (1)

(c) 0.5833 (1)

(ii) $\frac{8}{15}$ $\frac{4}{7}$ $\frac{7}{12}$ (1)

(iii) $\frac{1}{20}$ (3)

21 (i) 7 woodlice (1)   (iii) 7:5 (2)

(ii) $\frac{7}{12}$ (1)   (iv) 5:1 (1)

22 (a) (i) 72 boys (2)   (b) (i) 2:5 (2)

(ii) 48 girls (1)   (ii) 2:3 (2)

23 (a) 25 sweets (3)

(b) 5 kg (2)

24 (a) £17.50 (3)

(b) (i) 40°, 140°, 140°, 40° (4)

(ii) Isosceles trapezium (1)

25 (i) 20 sweets (2)

(ii) $2\frac{1}{2}m$ sweets (2)

(iii) (a) Morag 6 sweets; Hamish 15 sweets; 3 sweets left over. (2)

(b) 11 Jollys (2)

2 Calculations

2.1 Mental strategies

1	(a) £36	(1)	(d) £26.20	(1)
	(b) 5 goals	(1)	(e) £3.20	(1)
	(c) 15 kg	(1)		
2	(a) £240	(1)	(d) 48 boxes	(1)
	(b) 20 years old	(1)	(e) 4000 times	(1)
	(c) 3 m²	(1)		
3	(a) 27 points	(1)	(d) 480 ml	(1)
	(b) £140	(1)	(e) 41	(1)
	(c) £160	(1)		
4	(a) 25%	(1)	(d) 6 hectares	(1)
	(b) 70 grams	(1)	(e) 08:10	(1)
	(c) £90	(1)		
5	(a) 3	(1)	(d) £59.94	(1)
	(b) 14 degrees	(1)	(e) 26	(1)
	(c) 16 apples	(1)		
6	(a) $\frac{6}{13}$	(1)	(d) 25, 31, 44	(1)
	(b) 140°	(1)	(e) 39 cm	(1)
	(c) 20 chocolates	(1)		
7	(a) 120	(1)	(d) 1967	(1)
	(b) 16 children	(1)	(e) 29	(1)
	(c) £3.10	(1)		

8 (a) 20 bags (1)

(b) 2 min 53 s (1)

(c) 20 grams (1)

(d) 8th December (1)

(e) 2.5 m (1)

9 (a) 19:55 (1)

(b) £19 (1)

(c) 17 (1)

(d) 68 (1)

(e) Flag number 5 (1)

10 (a) $\frac{3}{7}$ (1)

(b) £99 (1)

(c) About 120 m (1)

(d) 12:12 (1)

(e) 2, 3 and 6 (1)

11 (a) 80p (1)

(b) 1995 (1)

(c) 9 (1)

(d) £9 (1)

(e) 630 g (1)

12 (a) £34.50 (1)

(b) 300° (1)

(c) $\frac{18}{30}$ (1)

(d) 50 minutes (1)

(e) 21 km (1)

13 (a) $\frac{1}{3}$ (1)

(b) £1.08 (1)

(c) 65° (1)

(d) 7200 minutes (1)

(e) 2:3 (1)

14 (a) 08:15 (1)

(b) 60 cm (1)

(c) 0.01 (1)

(d) 31 hours (1)

(e) 8 cm (1)

15 (a) 37 and 43 (1)

(b) 21 (the numbers are 21, 23 and 46 with a sum of 90) (1)

(c) 48 (1)

(d) 6 attempts (1)

(e) 6 (1)

16 (a) 12, 16   (1)   (d) $\frac{1}{3}$, $\frac{1}{2}$ (1)

    (b) 19 years old   (1)   (e) ⁻4   (1)

    (c) 15 years old   (1)

2.2 Written methods

It is expected that working is clearly set out.

1 (a) 6.399   (2)   (c) 2.875   (2)

  (b) 5.101   (2)   (d) 11.5   (2)

2 (a) 8.89   (2)   (c) 5.56   (2)

  (b) 2.17   (2)   (d) 1.67   (2)

3 (a) 38.1   (2)   (c) 15.52   (2)

  (b) 24.7   (2)   (d) 0.97   (2)

4 (a) 46.3   (1)   (c) 40   (1)

  (b) 2503   (2)   (d) 0.84   (2)

5 (a) 20.3   (2)   (c) 19.44   (2)

  (b) 7.34   (2)   (d) 2.16   (2)

6 (i) (a) $\frac{6}{7}$ (2)   (ii) $\frac{2}{7}$ (2)

    (b) $\frac{1}{3}$ (1)

7 (a) 7080   (2)   (b) Remainder 3   (2)

8 (a) 1   (2)   (b) 14   (2)

9 (a) £30   (2)   (c) £24.55   (2)

  (b) £11.95   (2)   (d) £12.40 and £6.20   (3)

10 (a) 11.63   (2)   (c) 47.18   (2)

   (b) 1.85   (2)   (d) 1.63   (2)

11 (a) 23.5   (2)   (c) 68   (2)

   (b) 3500   (2)

 **12** **(i)** **(a)** 5.72 (2)   **(ii)** 6.72 (2)

                (b) ⁻1 (2)

2.3 Calculator methods

1 **(i)** 0.380 952 381 (2)   **(iii)** 0.4 (1)

    (ii) 0.381 (1)

2 **(a)** **(i)** $\dfrac{400}{30+8}$ (2)   **(b)** **(i)** 10.687 635 57 (1)

        (ii) 11 (1)   **(ii)** 11 (1)

                                (iii) 10.7 (1)

3 **(a)** **(i)** 0.866 390 246 9 (2)

        (ii) 0.87 (1)

        (iii) 0.866 (1)

    (b) **(i)** $\dfrac{8000}{40\times20}$ (1)

        (ii) 10 (2)

4 **(a)** **(i)** 19.422 2 (2)   **(b)** 44.8 cm (2)

        (ii) 19.4 (1)

5 **(a)** **(i)** 43.217 777 78 (2)

        (ii) 43.218 (1)

        (iii) 43 (1)

    (b) 1 (3)

6 **(i)** 2.466 832 504 (2)   **(ii)** 2.47 (1)

7 **(i)** 6.71 (1)   **(ii)** 45 (1)

8 **(i)** 979.465 278 (2)   **(ii)** 980 (1)

9 **(i)** 3.189 945 652 (2)   **(iii)** 3.2 (1)

    (ii) 3.190 (1)

3 Problem solving

3.1 Reasoning about numbers or shapes

1 (i)   (2)

Year	Number of flowers
1	2
2	3
3	4
4	5
5	6

(ii) 8 flowers   (2)

(iii) Year 11   (2)

2 (i) (a) H   (1)

    (b) C   (1)

    (c) B and J   (1)

(ii) 9.4 cm²   (3)

3 (i) Fourth pattern drawn in the space on the dotted grid.   (1)

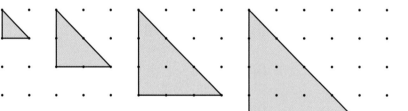

(ii)   (3)

Pattern number	1	2	3	4
Number of dots on perimeter	3	6	9	12
Number of dots inside pattern	0	0	1	3
Total number of dots	3	6	10	15

(iii) 18 dots   (1)

(iv) 15 dots   (2)

(v) 45 dots   (2)

4 (a) 720° (2)

   (b) (i) $18x$ (1)   (iii) $y = 20°$ (2)

      (ii) $x = 40°$ (2)   (iv) angle $BGE = 140°$ (2)

5 (i) $5x + 30 = 180$ (1)   (iii) angle $PBC = 40°$ (1)

  (ii) $x = 30°$ (3)   (iv) 9 sides (2)

6 (i) (a) $16 = 5 + 11$ or $16 = 3 + 13$ (1)

     (b) $28 = 5 + 23$ or $28 = 11 + 17$ (2)

     (c) $42 = 5 + 37$ or $42 = 11 + 31$ or $42 = 13 + 29$ or $42 = 19 + 23$ (2)

  (ii) $60 = 7 + 53$ (1)

     $60 = 13 + 47$ (1)

     $60 = 17 + 43$ (1)

     $60 = 19 + 41$ (1)

     $60 = 23 + 37$ (1)

     $60 = 29 + 31$ (1)

7 (a) 32 cm (2)

  (b) 49 cm² (1)

  (c) (i) $4x$ cm (1)   (iii) $x = 7$ (1)

     (ii) $10x$ cm (1)   (iv) Area = 196 cm² (1)

  (d) Area = 170 cm² (4)

8 (i) (a) $3A + B = 27$ (2)

     (b) $A + 2B = 24$ (2)

  (ii) $A = 6$; $B = 9$ (3)

  (iii) Puzzle completed (3)

				Row total
A	A	A	B	27
A	A	B	B	30
A	B	B	B	33
Column total 18	21	24	27	90

(iv) $30 = 2A + 2B$ or $30 = 5A$

$33 = 4A + B$ or $33 = A + 3B$

$36 = 3A + 2B$ or $36 = 6A$ or $36 = 4B$

$39 = 5A + B$ or $39 = 2A + 3B$ (3)

9 (i) 2, 5, 8, 11, 14   (2)   **(iii)** 100 cm   (2)

(ii) 23 cm   (1)   **(iv)** 59   (2)

10 (i)   (5)

Sixth term	27
Seventh term	51
Eighth term	6
Ninth term	36
Tenth term	39
Eleventh term	84
Twelfth term	24
Thirteenth term	18
Fourteenth term	65
Fifteenth term	31
Sixteenth term	4
Seventeenth term	16
Eighteenth term	37
Nineteenth term	52
Twentieth term	9
Twenty-first term	81
Twenty-second term	9
Twenty-third term	81

(ii) The sequence starts to repeat after the 20th term.   (2)

(iii) (a) 37, 52, 9, 81, 9, 81   (2)

      (b) 54, 21, 3, 9, 81, 9   (2)

11 (i) (a) $8x$ cm   (2)

      (b) 75 cm²   (2)

(ii) 99 cm²   (3)

12 (i) $\dfrac{3+4}{11}\left(\dfrac{7}{11}\right)$ (2)

(ii) $\dfrac{8}{99}$ (2)

13 (i) (3)

Macbeth	Macduff	Banquo
P	Q	R
P	Q	S
P	R	Q
P	R	S
P	S	Q
P	S	R
Q	R	S
Q	S	R
R	Q	S
R	S	Q
S	Q	R
S	R	Q

(ii) $\frac{5}{6}$ (2)

(iii) $\frac{1}{2}$ (2)

14 (i) **(a)** 3 layers (1)

(b) 10 coins (1)

(c) 35 coins (1)

(ii) (5)

Layer	Number of coins on an 'edge'	Number of coins in a layer	Total number of coins used so far
1 (top)	1	1	1
2	2	3	4
3	3	6	10
4	4	10	20
5	5	15	35
6	6	21	56
7	7	28	84
8	8	36	120
9	9	45	165
10	10	55	220

(III) **(a)** 3.15 cm (2)

(b) 2.09 kg (2)

15 (i) **(a)** 3 ways (1)

(b) 3 ways (1)

(c) 1 way (1)

(ii) (a) 1 way (1)

   (b) 4 ways (1)

   (c) 6 ways (2)

(iii) 20 ways (4)

16 (i)

n	n^3	$(n-1)^3$	$n^3-(n-1)^3$	digital root of $(n^3-(n-1)^3)$
1	1	0	1	1
2	8	1	7	7
3	27	8	19	1
4	64	27	37	1
5	125	64	61	7
6	216	125	91	1
7	343	216	127	1
8	512	343	169	7
9	729	512	217	1
10	1000	729	271	1

(8)

(ii) (a) The difference increases by 6 each time. (1)

   (b) Repeating sequence 1, 7, 1, 1, 7, 1, 1, 7, ... (1)

(iii) (a) 61 (2)

   (b) 169 (2)

(iv) Same as $n^3 - (n-1)^3$ (2)

(v) 29 701 (2)

17 (i) (a) Triangle *ABC* constructed. (2)

   (b) Angle bisectors constructed and point *D* marked. (2)

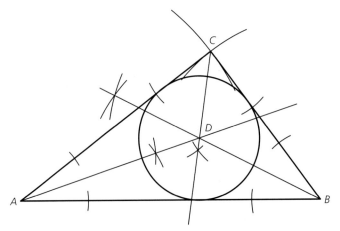

   (c) Inscribed circle, centre *D*, constructed. (1)

(ii) (a) Triangle *EFG* constructed. (2)

(b) Bisectors of sides constructed and point *H* marked. (2)

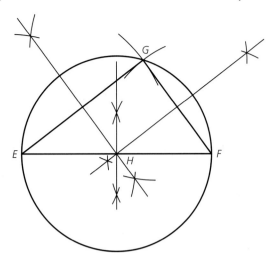

(c) Circumscribed circle, centre *H*, constructed. (1)

(d) *EF* is the diameter of the circle. (1)

18 (i) (a) Two congruent, obtuse-angled, scalene triangles, with sides 12 cm, 9 cm and 6 cm, constructed. (2)

(b) Inscribed circle of one triangle constructed. (2)

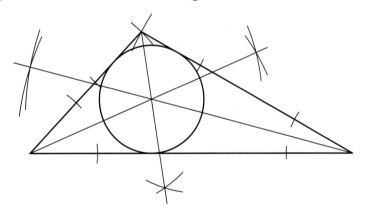

(c) Circumscribed circle of the second triangle constructed. (2)

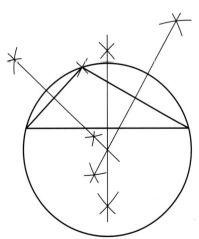

(ii) (a) Two congruent equilateral triangles, with sides 8 cm, constructed. (2)

(b) Inscribed circle of one triangle constructed. (2)

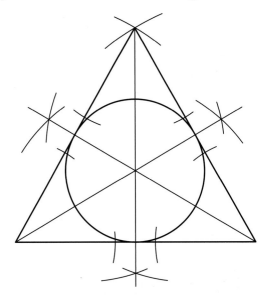

(c) Circumscribed circle of the second triangle constructed. (2)

(iii) Comments (2)

Comments may include:

- the point of intersection of the bisectors of the angles of any triangle is the centre of the inscribed circle

- the point of intersection of the perpendicular bisectors of the sides of any triangle is the centre of the circumscribed circle

- for an equilateral triangle, the bisectors of the angles and the perpendicular bisectors of the sides all intersect at the same point

- for an obtuse-angled scalene triangle, the centre of the circumscribed circle lies outside the triangle.

Questions 17 and 18 provide:

● a good challenge for accurate construction

● a starting point for an investigation.

19 (i) (a) CLXVI   (1)   (iv) (a) LXV   (1)

       (b) 166   (1)   (b) 65   (1)

   (ii) (a) IV   (1)   (v) (a) XVI   (1)

       (b) 4   (1)   (b) 16   (1)

  (iii) (a) LXIV   (1)

       (b) 64   (1)

3.2 Real-life mathematics

1 (i) £40   (2)   (ii) 45 litres   (2)

2 (a) £2.05   (2)   (c) £13.41   (2)

  (b) £5.51   (2)   (d) 4 rolls   (2)

3 (i) £216   (3)

  (ii) £225   (2)

  (iii) *Kilts4U* is cheaper by £9   (2)

  (iv) 40% of 360 > $\frac{1}{4}$ of 300   (1)

4 (i) (a) 54 km/h   (2)   (ii) 10.8 km   (2)

       (b) 15 m/s   (2)

5 (a) Chocolate   500 g

       Milk   1500 ml

       Cream   300 ml   (4)

  (b) 16 biscuits   (3)

6 (a) (i) 65 boys   (2)

     (ii) 5 : 9   (2)

(b) (i) A: regular pentagon (1)

    (ii) B: regular hexagon (1)

    (iii) Roller A turns through 72° (2)

    (iv) 3:2 (2)

    (v) 3:2 (2)

    (vi) $\frac{1}{6}$ (1)

7 (i) $\frac{11}{20}$ (3)   (iii) 2400 stamps (3)

  (ii) $\frac{11}{40}$ (2)

8 (i) 110 pence (or 111 pence) (3)

  (ii) 40 litres (or 39 litres) (2)

9 (i) 3 kg of parsnips at 45 pence per kg cost **135** pence

    6 kg of potatoes at **23** pence per kg cost 138 pence

    3 kg of sprouts at 68 pence per kg cost 204 pence

    The total amount spent on vegetables is £4.77 (4)

  (ii) 12 kg (1)

  (iii) 40 pence per kg (2)

10 £118 (3)

11 20°, 60°, 100° (2)

12 (i) 12 gallons (1)   (iii) £3 (2)

  (ii) 4 gallons (2)

13 (a) 4450 m (2)

  (b) (i) 3900 ml (2)

    (ii) 2.1 litres (1)

14 (a) £44 (2)

  (b) 20 km/h (2)

15 (i) $9 = 3 \times 3$; $16 = 2 \times 2 \times 2 \times 2$ (or with indices as $9 = 3^2$; $16 = 2^4$)   (2)

    (ii)   9, 18, 36, 72, 144   (2)

    (iii) (a)   3 pieces   (1)

       (b) $\frac{1}{6}$ (2)

    (iv)   20 g   (2)

    (v)   37.5%   (2)

16 (a) $\frac{9}{25}$ (2)   (c) (i)   £21.62   (2)

    (b)   0.125   (2)   (ii)   38.7%   (2)

17 (i)   13 miles per hour   (2)

    (ii) (a)   £55.25   (1)

       (b)   £92.25   (3)

18 945 km   (3)

19 (i)   16 290 cm²   (2)

    (ii) (a)   380 cm²   (1)

       (b)   88%   (3)

    (iii) 90 cm   (3)

20 (i)   3 m²   (3)   (iii) 95%   (3)

    (ii) 240 m²   (2)

21 (i)   (2)

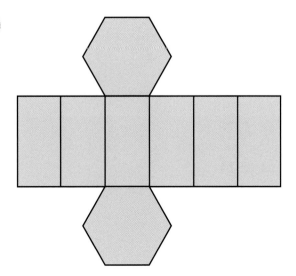

(ii) **(a)** Approximately 11 cm² (allow 10–12) (3)

 (b) Approximately 70 cm² (2)

22 (i) £225 (1) **(iii)** 44 hours (3)

 (ii) £326.20 (2)

23 (a) (i) £67.20 (2) **(b)** £180 (2)

 (ii) £63.84 (2)

 (iii) 33% (2)

24 (i) 84 pence (2)

 (ii) **(a)** A 90 pence, B 70 pence, C 95 pence (2)

 (b) £4.08 (3)

25 (i) Angela could get 4 small pizzas or 2 medium pizzas or 2 large pizzas. (2)

 (ii) Angela should get 4 small pizzas at a total cost of £9.90 (5)

26 (i) 4 hours 24 minutes (2)

 (ii) 220 km (2)

 (iii) 55 km/h (3)

27 (i) £13.50 (2) **(iii)** £6 (1)

 (ii) 9 DVDs (2) **(iv)** 8 DVDs (3)

28 (i) Debit, £249 (2) **(ii)** Credit, £151 (1)

29 (i) £60 (1)

 (ii) £45 (3)

 (iii) (a) £728 (2)

 (b) £624 (1)

 (iv) £812 (3)

Algebra

4.1 Equations and formulae

1. (i) $7a$ (1)
   (ii) $12a^2$ (2)
   (iii) $2a$ (2)
   (iv) ^-2a (2)

2. (i) $a - 3b$ (2)
   (ii) $12a^5$ (2)
   (iii) $\frac{1}{2}a$ (2)

3. (a) (i) a (2)
       (ii) $2a + 3b$ (2)
   (b) (i) $2x + y$ (2)
       (ii) $a + 3b$ (3)

4. (a) $5(n - 3)$ (2)
   (b) $p + 4q$ (3)

5. (a) $5m - 4n$ (2)
   (b) $6(2a + 3b)$ (2)

6. (a) $^-8$ (3)
   (b) $5(2u + 3)$ (2)

7. (a) $3x^2 + 5x - 2$ (2)
   (b) $6x^5$ (2)
   (c) $\frac{3}{x}$ (2)

8. (a) $10y - 1$ (2)
   (b) $5x$ (3)

9. (a) (i) $14a + 35$ (1)
       (ii) $4a + 2$ (2)
   (b) (i) $2(3a + 5)$ (2)
       (ii) $4b(2a - 3c)$ (2)

10. (i) $6p^2 - 13p^3$ (2)
    (ii) $^-2h + 30$ (2)
    (iii) $\frac{1}{2}$ (2)

11. (a) (i) $4y^3$ (1)
        (ii) $4y^6$ (2)
        (iii) $\frac{4}{y^4}$ (2)
    (b) $p - 30q$ (3)
    (c) $5a(3a + 5)$ (2)

12 (a) $3a + 8$ (3)

(b) $4(2a - 3b)$ (2)

(c) (i) $a^3 + 5a^2$ (2) **(iii)** $\dfrac{3}{2a}$ (2)

(ii) $24a^9$ (2)

13 (a) $3(1 - 12y)$ (2) **(b)** $2x$ (2)

14 (i) $9a^2 - 2ab$ (2) **(iii)** $11x$ (3)

(ii) 5 (3)

15 (i) 8 (1) **(iv)** 16 (2)

(ii) 1 (1) **(v)** $^-35$ (2)

(iii) 6 (2)

16 (i) 13 (2) **(iii)** 9 (2)

(ii) $^-3$ (2) **(iv)** $^-24$ (2)

17 (i) 6 (2) **(iii)** 25 (2)

(ii) 4 (2)

18 (i) 11 (2) **(iii)** 9 (2)

(ii) $^-3$ (2)

19 (i) 1 (2) **(iii)** 6 (2)

(ii) 0 (2)

20 (i) 18 (1) **(iii)** $^-3$ (3)

(ii) 12 (2)

21 (i) $^-\dfrac{1}{4}$ (2) **(iii)** 4 (2)

(ii) $^-\dfrac{1}{6}$ (2)

22 (i) 390 (1) **(iii)** 575.9 (1)

(ii) 185.9 (1)

23 (i) $(x + 1)$ cm   (1)   **(iv)** 25 cm   (1)

    (ii) $(8x + 4)$ cm   (3)   **(v)** 225 cm²   (2)

    (iii) $x = 8$ (2)

24 (i) **(a)** $(4x + 12)$ cm   (2)   **(ii)** $x = 3$ (4)

    (b) $(4x - 10)$ cm   (2)

25 (i) $(x + 8)$ cm   (1)   **(iv)** $x = 4$ (3)

    (ii) $4x$ cm   (1)   **(v)** 12 cm   (1)

    (iii) $(6x + 8)$ cm   (2)

26 (i) $3x$ cm   (1)   **(iv)** $5(x + 1)$ (1)

    (ii) $(x + 5)$ cm   (1)   **(v)** $x = 5$ (3)

    (iii) $(5x + 5)$ cm   (2)

27 (i) $n + 5$ (1)   **(iii)** 17 years old   (2)

    (ii) $n = 9$ (2)

28 (i) $8b$ pence   (1)   **(iii)** bx pence   (1)

    (ii) $z - 8b$ pence   (1)   **(iv)** $500 - bx - cy$ pence   (2)

29 (i) (7)

	Peter	Quentin	Rachel
At the start	x	$x + 4$	$x - 2$
Game 1: Peter loses 2 to Quentin	$x - 2$	$x + 6$	$x - 2$
Game 2: Peter loses 4 to Rachel	$x - 6$	$x + 6$	$x + 2$
Game 3: Quentin loses 1 to Rachel	$x - 6$	$x + 5$	$x + 3$

    (ii) $x = 9$ (3)

    (iii) They have 29 marbles altogether.

    Peter has 3 marbles; Quentin has 14 marbles; Rachel has 12 marbles.   (2)

30 (i) $a = 8$ (1)   **(iii)** $c = 6$ (1)

    (ii) $b = 11$ (1)   **(iv)** $d = 4$ (2)

31 (i) $x = 2$ (1)   **(iii)** $z = 1\frac{1}{2}$ (2)

    (ii) $y = {}^-2$ (2)

32 (i) $a = 4$ (2)   **(iii)** $c = 2$ (2)

(ii) $b = 24$ (1)   **(iv)** $d = 4$ (1)

33 (i) $a = 18$ (1)   **(iii)** $c = 3$ (3)

(ii) $b = 2$ (2)   **(iv)** $d = 4\frac{1}{3}$ (2)

34 (i) $x = 1$ (2)   **(iii)** $z = {}^-1$ (3)

(ii) $y = \frac{2}{7}$ (3)

35 (i) $x = {}^-1$ (1)   **(iii)** $z = 6$ (2)

(ii) $y = 2\frac{1}{2}$ (2)

36 (i) $y = 3\frac{1}{2}$ (1)   **(iii)** $z = 7$ (2)

(ii) $x = {}^-2$ (1)

37 (i) $r = 9$ (2)   **(iii)** $s = \frac{1}{4}$ (3)

(ii) $q = {}^-1$ (2)

38 (i) $a = 4$ (2)   **(iii)** $c = 25$ (2)

(ii) $b = {}^-18$ (2)   **(iv)** $d = 50$ (2)

39 (i) $u = 8$ (2)   **(iv)** $x = {}^-24$ (3)

(ii) $v = 7$ (2)   **(v)** $y = \frac{4}{9}$ (3)

(iii) $w = 12$ (3)

40 (a) $x = 32$ (2)   **(c)** $x < 1\frac{1}{2}$ (3)

(b) ${}^-4, {}^-3, {}^-2, {}^-1$ (3)

41 (a) (i) $x = 72$ (1)   **(b)** 11, 12, 13 (3)

(ii) $y = 2\frac{1}{2}$ (3)

(iii) $z = 3$ (2)

42 (a) 1, 2, 3, 4 (3)   **(b)** $x > 5$ (3)

43 (a) (i) $p < 2\frac{2}{3}$ (2)   **(b) (i)** $q \leq 15$ (3)

(ii) 1, 2 (1)   **(ii)** $q = 15$ (1)

44 (i) (a) $x \le 8$ (2)   (ii) 2, 3, 5, 7 (1)

(b) $x > {}^-2$ (2)

45 (a) $x = 27$ (2)   (c) $2c(c + 2d)$ (2)

(b) $t < 5$ (3)   (d) $2\frac{1}{2}$ (2)

46 (a) (i) $x = {}^-1$ (2)   (b) (i) $12x^3 y^2$ (3)

(ii) $x = 8$ (3)   (ii) 1 (2)

(iii) $2x$ (3)

47 $x = 7.8$ Completed tables may vary. (4)

48 $x = 6.2$ (5)

49 $x = 1.32$ (5)

50 (i) (a) $w + 1.2$ (1)   (ii) (a) 15 cm (4)

(b) $w(w + 1.2)$ (2)   (b) 62.4 cm (2)

51 (i) (a) $s - 3.5$ (1)   (ii) 4.5, 8 (3)

(b) $s(s - 3.5)$ (2)

4.2 Sequences and functions

1 (a) (i) 31, 27 (2)   (b) 6, 16 (2)

(ii) 21, 31 (2)

(iii) 50, 25 (2)

2 (i) 12, 7 (1)   (iii) 15, 21 (2)

(ii) 16, 32 (2)   (iv) $\frac{7}{12}, \frac{1}{2}$ (2)

3 (a) (i) $\frac{1}{4}$, 0.3 (2)

(ii) 62, 126 (2)

(iii) 125, 216 (2)

(b) Examples:

4, 5 because it is the sequence of counting numbers

5, 8 because the next term is the sum of the two previous terms. (2)

4 **(i)** 30, 37 (2)   **(iii)** 3, $3\frac{1}{2}$ (2)

  (ii) 81, 243 (2)

5 **(a)** **(i)** 7, 10 (2)   **(b)** 3, 11, 123 (2)

     (ii) 111, 161 (2)

    (iii) 5, 50 (2)

6 **(a)** **(i)** 2.25, 2.5, 2.75 (2)   **(b)** **(i)** 1 (2)

     (ii) 15 (2)   **(ii)** $5\frac{1}{2}$ (2)

    (iii) 4 terms (2)   **(iii)** $10\frac{1}{2}$ (2)

                    (iv) 50 (2)

7 **(i)** 17, 21 (1)   **(iii)** $4n - 3$ (2)

  (ii) 37 (1)   **(iv)** 26 (2)

8 **(i)** 50, 72, 98, 128 (4)   **(iii)** $A_n = n$ (1)

  (ii) $n = 20$ (3) $B_n = 2n$ (1)

                                     $C_n = 2n^2$ (2)

9 **(i)** **(a)** $t_1 = 0$, $t_2 = 2$, $t_3 = 6$ and $t_4 = 12$ (2)

     (b) $t_{20} = 380$ (1)

  (ii) **(a)** $t_5 = 0 + 2 + 4 + 6 + 8 = 20$ (1)

     (b) 110 (2)

 (iii) Dot patterns drawn for t_5 (2)

 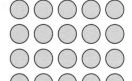

10 Lines drawn and labelled.

    (i) $x = 5$ (1)

    (ii) $y = {}^-3$ (1)

    (iii) $y = x$ (2)

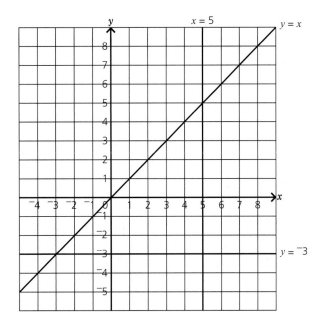

11 (i) **(a)** Multiplies by 2   (1)

           (b) Adds 3   (1)

    (ii) **(a)** 17   (1)

           (b) 10   (2)

    (iii) **(a)** 20   (1)

           (b) $8\frac{1}{2}$ (2)

12 (i) Adds 9   (1)

    (ii)   (2)

Input	Output
4	21
11	42

13 (i)   (2)

x	0	2	4
y	${}^-1$	1	3

    (ii) Line $y = x - 1$ drawn on grid.   (2)

(iii) Suitable values used to complete the table; for example:

x	0	2	4
y	10	8	6

Line $y = 10 - x$ drawn on grid. (3)

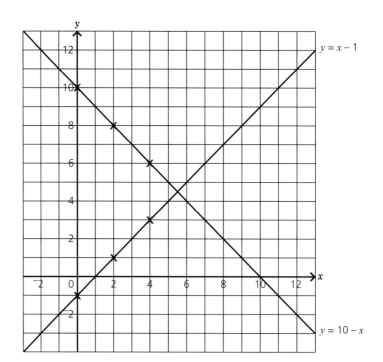

(iv) $\left(5\frac{1}{2}, 4\frac{1}{2}\right)$ (1)

14 (i) (3)

Input	Output
1	4
2	7
4	13

(ii) $y = 3x + 1$ (2)

15 (i)

Input	Output	
0	1	(1)
1	2	(1)
2	5	(1)
3	10	(1)
7	50	(2)

(ii) $y = x^2 + 1$ (2)

16 (i) (3)

x	−2	−1	0	1	2	3
y	2	−1	−2	−1	2	7

(ii) Points plotted and curve drawn. (3)

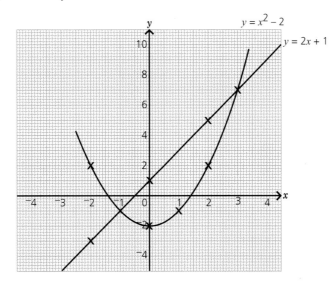

(iii)

x	$^-2$	0	2
y	$^-3$	1	5

Line drawn (see previous grid). (3)

(iv) $(^-1, ^-1)$ and $(3, 7)$ (2)

17 (i) $y = x^2 + 4$ (2)   **(ii)** $\left(\frac{1}{2}, 4\frac{1}{4}\right)$ (2)

In questions 18 to 25, readings from the graphs will, in most cases, be approximate and dependent upon the accuracy of drawing the graphs of the quadratic functions. Credit should be given for answers which are close to those provided.

18 (i) Graph drawn. (2)

(ii) (2)

x	$^-2$	0	2	4
y	1	3	5	7

(iii) Graph of $y = x + 3$ drawn. (1)

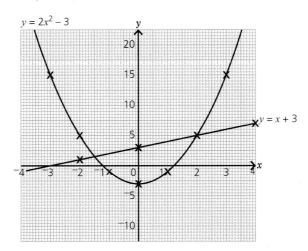

(iv) $(2, 5)$ and $(^-1.5, 1.5)$ (2)

19 $y = \dfrac{x^2}{4}$

x	⁻2	⁻1	0	1	2	3	4
y	1	$\frac{1}{4}$	0	$\frac{1}{4}$	1	$2\frac{1}{4}$	4

$y = x$

x	⁻2	⁻1	0	1	2	3	4
y	⁻2	⁻1	0	1	2	3	4

(0, 0) and (4 , 4)   (4)

20 (i)   (5)

x	⁻3	⁻2	⁻1	0	1	2	3	4
y	⁻0.5	2	3.5	4	3.5	2	⁻0.5	⁻4

(ii) Graph of $y = 4 - \frac{1}{2}x^2$ drawn.   (3)

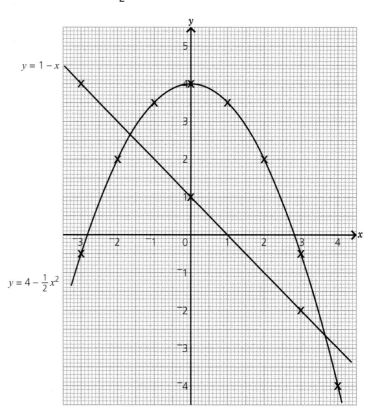

(iii)   (1)

x	⁻3	0	3
y	4	1	⁻2

(iv) Line $y = 1 - x$ drawn on the grid.   (2)

(v) (⁻1.7, 2.7) and (3.7, ⁻2.7)   (2)

21 (i)   (2)

x	⁻2	⁻1	0	1	2	3	4
y	0	⁻3	⁻4	⁻3	0	5	12

(ii) Curve drawn. (3)

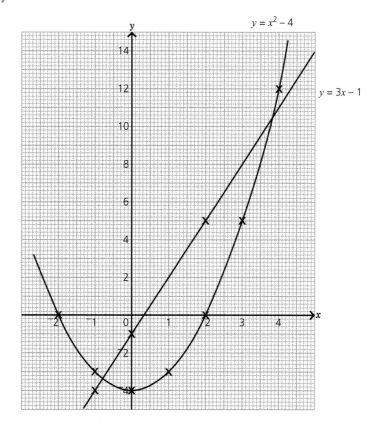

(iii) (2)

x	⁻1	0	2
y	⁻4	⁻1	5

(iv) Line $y = 3x - 1$ drawn. (2)

(v) (⁻0.8, ⁻3.4) and (3.8, 10.4) (2)

22 (i) (3)

x	⁻3	⁻2	⁻1	0	1	2	3
y	6	1	⁻2	⁻3	⁻2	1	6

(ii) Graph of $y = x^2 - 3$ drawn. (3)

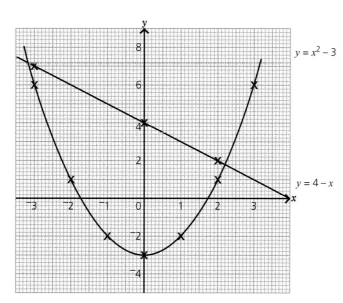

(iii)

x	-3	0	2
y	7	4	2

(2)

(iv) Graph of $y = 4 - x$ drawn.

(1)

(v) (-3.2, 7.2) and (2.2, 1.8)

(2)

23 (i) (a)

x	-2	-1	0	1	2
y	7	4	3	4	7

(2)

(b) Graph of $y = x^2 + 3$ drawn.

(3)

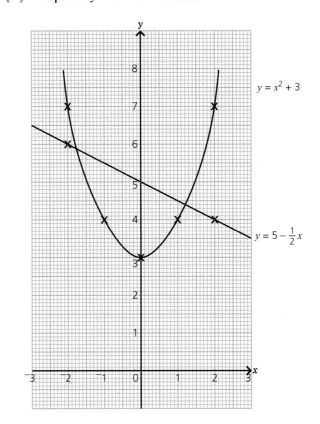

(ii) (a)

x	-2	0	2
y	6	5	4

(2)

(b) Graph of $y = 5 - \frac{1}{2}x$ drawn.

(2)

(iii) (1.2, 4.4)

(2)

24 (i)

x	-3	-2	-1	0	1	2	3
y	14	4	-2	-4	-2	4	14

(3)

(ii) Graph of $y = 2x^2 - 4$ drawn. (2)

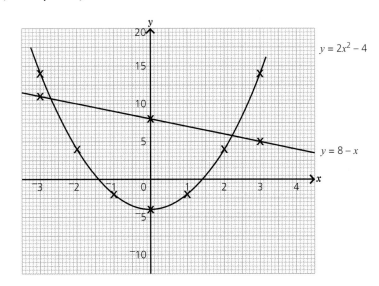

(iii) (2)

x	$^-3$	0	3
y	11	8	5

(iv) Graph of $y = 8 - x$ drawn. (1)

(v) $(^-2.7, 10.7)$ and $(2.2, 5.8)$ (2)

25 (i) (3)

x	$^-3$	$^-2$	$^-1$	0	1	2	3
y	$^-5$	0	3	4	3	0	$^-5$

(ii) Graph of $y = 4 - x^2$ drawn. (2)

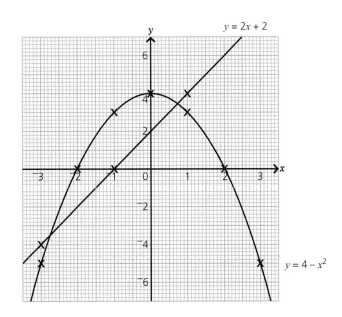

(iii) (2)

x	$^-3$	$^-1$	1
y	$^-4$	0	4

(iv) Graph of $y = 2x + 2$ drawn. (1)

(v) ($^-$2.75, $^-$3.5) and (0.75, 3.5) (2)

26 (i) $4x + 3y = 170$ (1)

(ii) $3x = 2y$ (1)

(iii) $x = 20, y = 30$ (4)

(iv) 10 oranges, 7 oranges and 2 lemons, 4 oranges and 4 lemons, 1 orange and 6 lemons (3)

27 (i) $x = \dfrac{7y}{2}$ (1)

(ii) $x = 3y + 2$ (1)

(iii) $x = 14, y = 4$ (4)

(iv) 7:1 (2)

28 $a = 23, b = 4$ (4)

29 (i) $5(x + y) = 80$ or $x + y = 16$
$x - y = 7$ (3)

(ii) $x = 11\frac{1}{2}, y = 4\frac{1}{2}$ (3)

30 (i) (a) $l - w$ (1)

(b) $2(l + w)$ or $2l + 2w$ (2)

(ii) $l - w = 6, 2(l + w) = 42$
$l = 13.5\,\text{cm}, w = 7.5\,\text{cm}$ (3)

(iii) 101.25 cm² (1)

5 Geometry and measures

5.1 Measures

1	(i)	2 pounds	(2)	(ii)	45 kg	(3)
2	(i)	1.27 m	(2)	(ii)	79 inches	(2)
3	(a)	(i) 20 ha				(1)
		(ii) 49.4 acres				(2)
	(b)	1000 m²				(3)
4	(i)	Answers will vary; for example:				(3)

	Estimate
Length	35 cm
Width	30 cm
Depth	12 cm
Volume	12 600 cm³

	(ii)	10 litres				(2)
5	(i)	60 g				(2)
	(ii)	20 cm				(2)
	(iii)	110 cm³				(2)
6	(i)					(3)

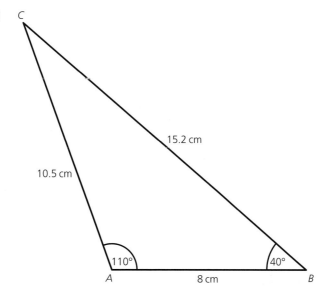

      (ii)   Approximately 33.7 cm   (2)

7 (i) 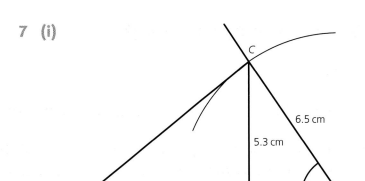 (3)

(ii) 5.3 cm (2)

(iii) Angle $BCA = 86°$ (2)

8 (a) (i) Line *AB*, 10.8 cm, drawn. (2)

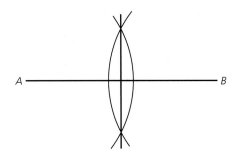

(ii) Perpendicular bisector of *AB* constructed. (2)

(b) (i) (3)

(ii) 28.4 cm (2)

9 (i) Kite constructed. (4)

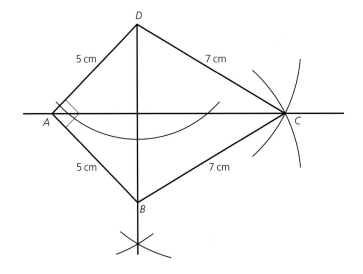

(ii) Line of symmetry drawn through *AC*. (1)

(iii) Kite (1)

(iv) Perpendicular to *AC* passing through *D* constructed. (2)

(v) The perpendicular extended passes through *B* (reinforcing the fact that the diagonals of a kite intersect at right angles). (1)

10 (i) Rhombus *ABCD* constructed. (3)

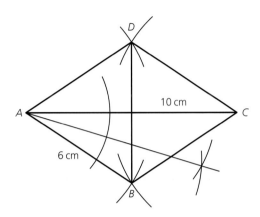

(ii) 6.5 cm (1)

(iii) 32.5 cm² (2)

(iv) Bisector of angle *BAC* constructed. (2)

11 (i) 30°, 90°, 150°, 90° (2)

(ii) (3)

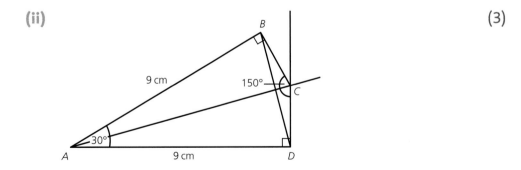

(iii) Approximately 22 cm² (3)

12 (i) Trapezium (1)

(ii) 6.3 cm² (4)

13 (i) (3)

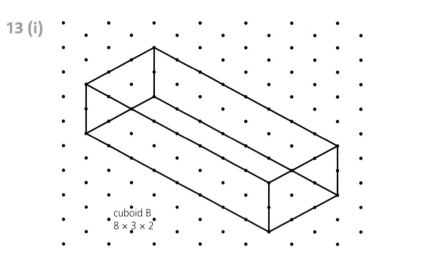

cuboid B
8 × 3 × 2

Other possible answers include 4 × 4 × 3, 2 × 2 × 12, etc.

(ii) 88 cm² (4)

14 (i) 1125 cm³ (4)

(ii) 525 cm² (4)

15 (i) Cuboid drawn. (2)

(ii) 180 cm³ (1)

(iii) Shape of the hole drawn on the diagram. (2)

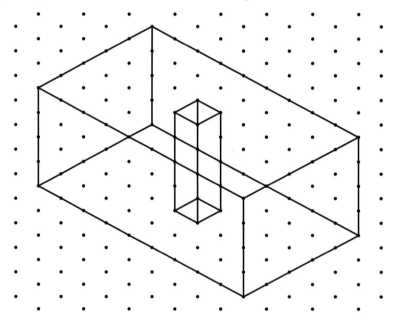

(iv) 200 cm² (4)

16 (i) 1:16 (2)

(ii) 1:64 (2)

17 (i) 320 m — (2)

(ii) 0.64 hectares — (2)

18 (i) 0.950 m² — (2) **(iii)** 3 tins — (3)

(ii) 0.238 m² — (2)

19 (i) 21 344 km — (3)

(ii) 21 300 km — (1)

20 (i) (a) 25.1 cm — (2)

(b) 50.3 cm² — (3)

(ii) (a) 37.7 cm — (2)

(b) Height of triangle 6.93 ($\sqrt{48}$), so area is $\frac{1}{2} \times 8 \times 6.93$, giving 27.71... — (3)

(c) 103 cm² — (2)

21 (i) (a) 188 cm — (2) **(ii)** (a) 154 cm — (2)

(b) 2827 cm² — (2) (b) 157 cm² — (2)

(c) 283 cm³ — (2)

22 (i) 1.85 m — (2) **(iii)** 56.8 cm — (2)

(ii) 54 revolutions — (2)

23 (a) 15 : 13 — (2)

(b) 2 hours 23 minutes — (2)

(c) (i) 4 minutes — (1)

(ii) 7 km — (1)

(d) (i) 7200 m — (1)

(ii) 2 m/s — (2)

24 (i) 2.5 m/s — (2) **(iii)** 5 seconds — (1)

(ii) 25 seconds — (2) **(iv)** 10 m — (2)

1 (i) Points plotted and joined to form *PQRS*. (3)

(ii) Lines of symmetry drawn. (2)

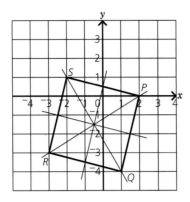

(iii) Order 4 (1)

2 (i)

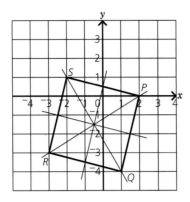

The quadrilateral is an isosceles trapezium. (2)

(ii)

The quadrilateral is a parallelogram. (2)

3 (i) 45° (2)

(ii) 135° (2)

(iii) 90° (2)

4 (i) (a) 36° (2)

(b) 144° (2)

(ii) Isosceles trapezium (1)

(iii) 108° (2)

5 (i) Order 18 (1)

(ii) 20° (2)

(iii) 2880° (2)

(iv) 140° (2)

(v) Isosceles trapezium (1)

6 (i) Hexagonal prism (3)

(ii) 12 ways (2)

7 (i) (3)

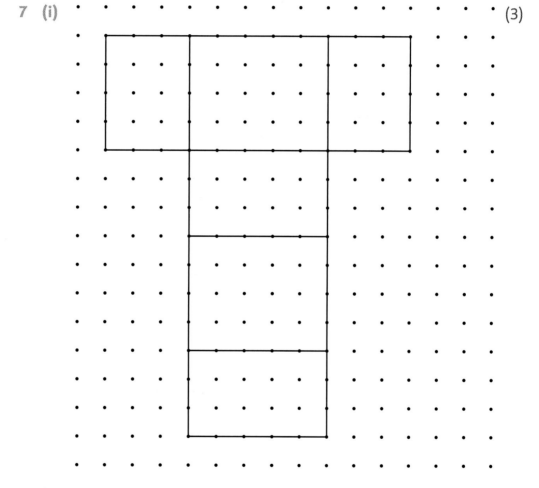

(ii) 94 cm² (3)

(iii) 60 cm³ (1)

5.3 Space

1 (i) $a = 50°$ (1) (iii) $c = 40°$ (2)

(ii) $b = 130°$ (2)

2 (i) $a = 54°$ (1)   (iii) $c = 117°$ (2)

   (ii) $b = 63°$ (2)

3 (a) (i) $a = 72°$ (1)   (b) (i) $p = 105°$ (1)

       (ii) $b = 76°$ (1)   (ii) $q = 120°$ (1)

       (iii) $c = 32°$ (2)   (iii) $r = 150°$ (2)

4 (a) (i) $a = 62°$ (1)   (b) (i) $d = 70°$ (1)

       (ii) $b = 31°$ (2)   (ii) $e = 42°$ (2)

       (iii) $c = 149°$ (2)

5 (a) (i) $a = 28°$ (1)   (b) $d = 60°$ (2)

       (ii) $b = 76°$ (2)

       (iii) $c = 104°$ (2)

6 (i) 108° (2)   (iii) 192° (2)

   (ii) 36° (2)

7 (i) 1260° (3)

   (ii) (a) $60x°$ (2)

        (b) $x = 21°$ (2)

        (c) 105° (1)

8 (i) (4)

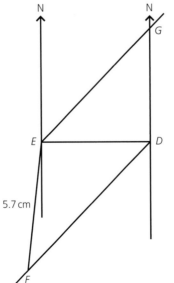

(ii) (a) Approximately 11.4 m   (2)

  (b) North-east   (2)

9 (i) Scale drawing with position of *B*.   (3)

  (ii) *A′* plotted   (2)

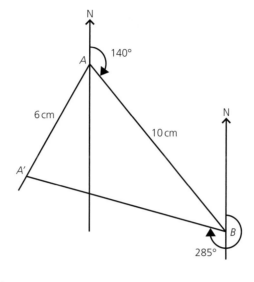

  (iii) 49 m   (1)

  (iv) 285°   (2)

10 (i) Scale drawing with *T* plotted.   (3)

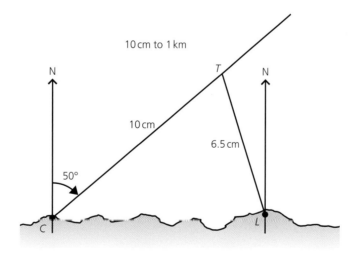

  (ii) (a) 650 m   (2)

   (b) 342°   (2)

  (iii) 3 minutes   (2)

11 (i) Lines drawn to show position of Y.   (3)

(The shape of the lake may vary in pupil copies.)

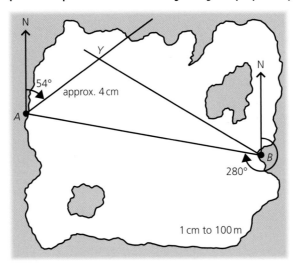

    (ii) 420 m (accept approx. 400 m)   (2)

    (iii) 280°   (2)

12 (i) Diagram drawn to show the positions of W and P.   (4)

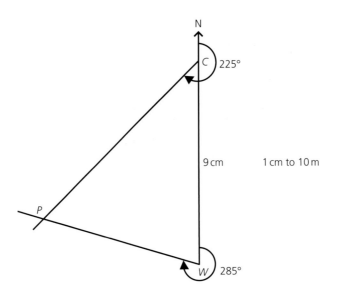

    (ii) 74 m   (2)

13 (i) 1 km   (1)

    (ii) Bratby marked on diagram.   (2)

    (iii) 250°   (1)

(iv) Creakybridge marked. (3)

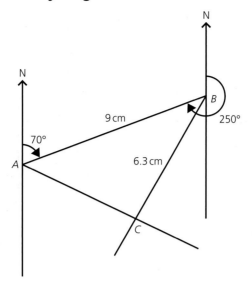

(v) 6.3 km (2)

14 (i) **(a)** Line $x = 4$ (1)

  (b) Triangle **B** (2)

(ii) Triangle **C** (2)

(iii) Triangle **D** (2)

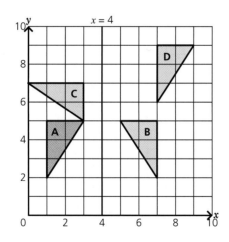

(iv) 3 units² (1)

15 (i) Points plotted. (1)

(ii) Points joined to form triangle **A**. (1)

(iii) Triangle **B** (2)

(iv) Triangle **C** (2)

(v) Reflect in the line $y = 2$ (2)

(vi) Triangle **D** (2)

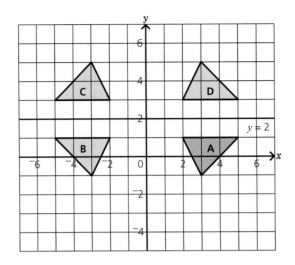

16 (i) Triangle **A** (2)

   (ii) **(a)** Line $x = 2$ (1)

   (b) Triangle **B** (2)

(iii) Triangle **C** (3)

(iv) Triangle **D** (1)

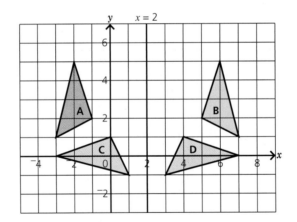

17 (i) Points plotted. (1)

   (ii) Triangle **A** (1)

   (iii) Triangle **B** (2)

   (iv) Triangle **C** (2)

   (v) Mirror line (1)

(vi) $y = {}^{-}x\ (x + y = 0)$ (1)

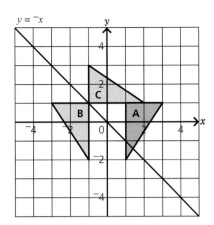

18 (2)

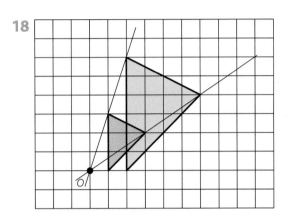

19 (i) Triangle **B** (3)

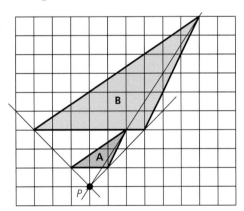

(ii) 2 cm² (2)

(iii) 18 cm² (2)

20 (i) Points plotted. (2)

(ii) Parallelogram (1)

(iii) *A' B' C' D'* (2)

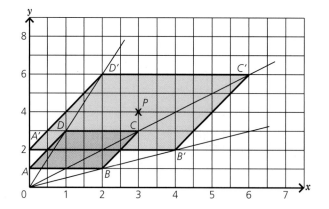

(iv) (3, 4) (1)

(v) 4:1 (2)

21 (i) Shape **A** (2)

(ii) Shape **B** (3)

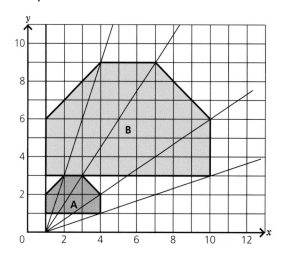

(iii) 45 cm² (3)

22 (i) Triangle **A** (1)

(ii) Triangle **B** (2)

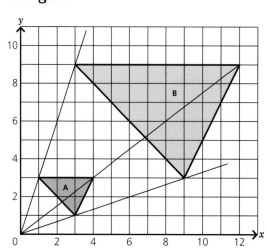

(iii) 9 triangles (2)

23 (i) (3)

(ii) 14 cm² (2)

(iii) $3\frac{1}{2}$ cm² (2)

24 (i) (a) 7.5 cm (2)   (ii) 81 cm² (3)

(b) 18 cm (2)

25 (i) 5 m (2)   (iii) 25.8 m (2)

(ii) 2.4 m (2)   (iv) 84 m³ (3)

26 (i) 5 cm (2)

(ii) 24 cm² (2)

27 106° and 74° (4)

28 (a) (i) 15.6 cm (2)   (b) (i) 90° (1)

(ii) 50.7 cm² (2)   (ii) 3.35 cm (2)

(iii) 22.6° (3)   (iii) 3.72 cm (2)

(iv) 6.23 cm² (2)

6 Statistics and probability

6.1 Statistics

1 (i) (3)

Type of coin	Tally	Frequency
5p	卌 I	6
10p	卌	5
20p	卌	5
50p	IIII	4
	Total	20

(ii) 5p (1) **(iv)** 380p (2)

(iii) 10p (2) **(v)** 19p (2)

2 (i) (a) 103 (1)

(b) 630 sweets (1)

(ii) 21 sweets (2)

(iii) (3)

Number of sweets	Tally	Frequency
18	I	1
19	卌	5
20	卌 I	6
21	卌	5
22	卌 II	7
23	卌 I	6

(iv) 22 (1)

3 (i) (4)

Mark awarded	1	2	3	4	5	6	7	8	9	10
Number of children	0	0	2	1	2	1	1	4	5	4

(ii) 9 (1) **(v)** 7.5 marks (1)

(iii) 8 (3) **(vi)** It sounds better! (1)

(iv) 150 marks (2)

4 (i) 40 children (1) **(iii)** 15% (2)

(ii) $\frac{3}{10}$ (2) **(iv)** $\frac{9}{20}$ (2)

5 (i) 40 peas (2)   (iii) 4 peas (2)

   (ii) 3 m (1)   (iv) $\frac{1}{10}$ (1)

6 (i) (a) 613 (2)

     (b) 61.3% (2)

   (ii) (a) 658 (1)

     (b) 85% (3)

   (iii) English 2, Science, French, Spanish, Geography, Religious Studies (3)

7 (i) 344 kg (2)   (iii) 52 kg (2)

   (ii) 240 kg (1)

8 (i) (a) 3.8 seconds (1)   (ii) (a) 7.09 m/s (2)

     (b) 15.4 seconds (2)   (b) 25.5 km/h (2)

     (c) 15.7 seconds (2)

9 (i) 5% (1)

   (ii) (a) 36° (1)

     (b) 18° (1)

   (iii) (3)

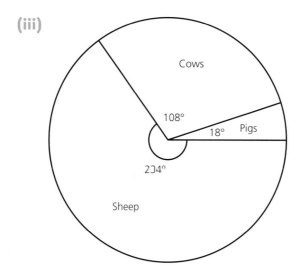

10 (i) 5° (2)   (iii) 11 children (2)

   (ii) 35° (2)

11 (i) 5% (2)   (iii) 72° (3)

   (ii) 54 pages (2)

12 (i) 6 hours (2)   **(iii)** 54° (2)

   (ii) 13 hours 12 minutes (2)

13 (i) 60 girls (2)

   (ii) 90° sector for netball drawn and labelled. (2)

 (iii) Sectors for swimming and tennis drawn and labelled. (4)

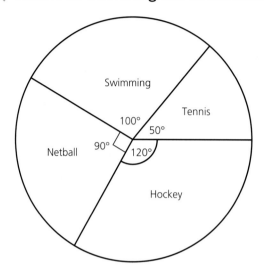

14 (i) 18 people (1)

   (ii) (4)

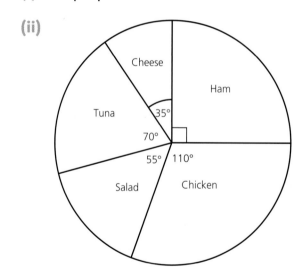

15 (i) (3)

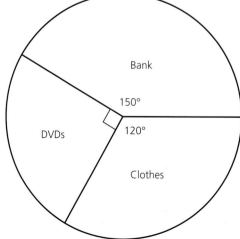

(ii) £6.25 (2)

(iii) £7.75 (3)

16 (i) (a) 4 degrees (2)

   (b) 7 °C (1)

(ii) (a) 7.5 °C (2)

   (b) 7.9 °C (2)

(iii) (2)

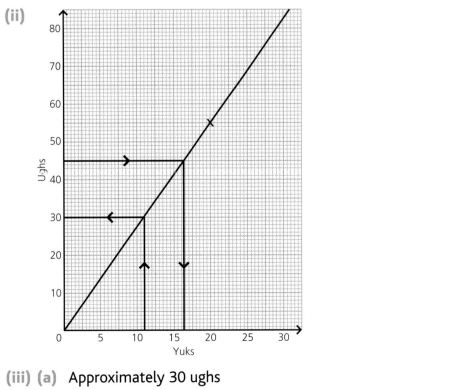

17 (i) The graph passes through the reference points (0, **0**) and
(250, **100**). (1)

(ii) 104 inches (2)

(iii) 175 cm (3)

18 (i) 55 ughs (2)

(ii) (3)

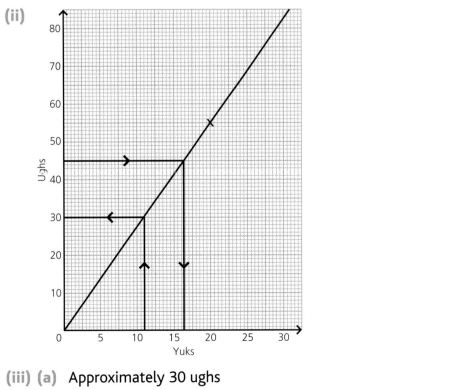

(iii) (a) Approximately 30 ughs (1)

   (b) Approximately 16.5 yuks (1)

19 (i) 12.5 g (2)

(ii) (5)

	1 biscuit	100 g	250 g packet
Number of biscuits	1	8	20
Mass (g)	12.5	100	250
Energy (calories)	60	480	1200

20 (i) 40 litres (2)

(ii) (2)

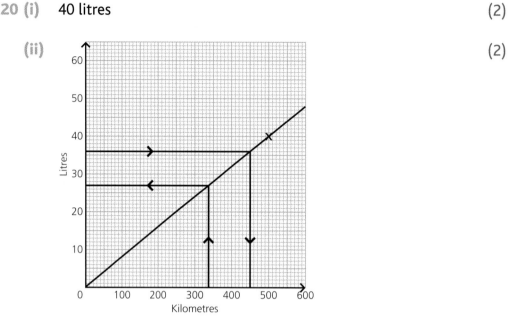

(iii) (a) 450 km (2)

(b) 10 litres (2)

21 (i) High, positive correlation (1)

(ii) One – the point is circled on the diagram below. (1)

(iii) The line of best fit passes through (or very close to) the points (55, **55**) and (90, **80**). (2)

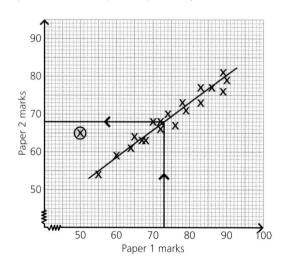

(iv) About 68 (2)

22 (i) Results plotted. (3)

(ii) Line of best fit drawn. (1)

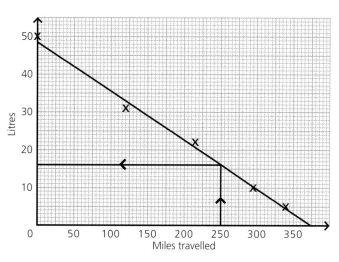

(iii) Approximately 34 litres (2)

(iv) Approximately 375 miles (2)

23 Low, positive correlation up to the age of about 40

Low, negative correlation after the age of about 40 (3)

24 (i) (a) 34 inches (1)

(b) 14 inches (1)

(c) Size $9\frac{1}{2}$ (2)

(ii) (a) Scatter diagram drawn. (5)

(b) Line of best fit drawn. (1)

(c) Positive correlation. (2)

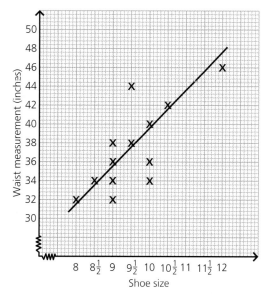

(iii) $\frac{2}{7}$ (2)

1 (i) Left blue and right green

Left blue and left green

Left blue and right blue

Right blue and right green

Right blue and left green

Left green and right green (3)

(ii) (a) $\frac{1}{6}$ (1)

(b) $\frac{1}{3}$ (1)

2 (i) (3)

Goalkeeper	Sweeper
P	Q
P	R
P	S
Q	R
Q	S
R	Q
R	S
S	Q
S	R

(ii) $\frac{5}{9}$ (2)

(iii) $\frac{3}{5}$ (2)

3 (a) (i) (1)

		First bag		
		1p	2p	5p
Second bag	1p	1p, 1p	2p, 1p	5p, 1p
	5p	1p, 5p	2p, 5p	5p, 5p

(ii) 3 pairs (1) **(iv)** $\frac{1}{3}$ (1)

(iii) $\frac{1}{2}$ (1) **(v)** $\frac{2}{3}$ (1)

(b) (i) $\frac{1}{5}$ (2)

(ii) $\frac{7}{30}$ (2)

4 (i) Letter A (1) **(ii)** Letter B (1) **(iii)** Letter C (4)

5 (a) (i) $\frac{5}{18}$ (1)   (b) (i) $\frac{1}{2}$ (1)

     (ii) $\frac{2}{3}$ (2)   (ii) Even chance (1)

6 (i) $\frac{1}{5}$ (2)   (ii) $\frac{3}{20}$ (2)

7 (i) $\frac{1}{5}$ (1)   (iii) $\frac{2}{3}$ (2)

   (ii) $\frac{7}{10}$ (2)

8 (i) (a) $\frac{1}{22}$ (1)   (ii) $\frac{1}{9}$ (2)

     (b) $\frac{7}{22}$ (1)

9 (i) (a) Set A: {30, 32, 34, 36, 38, 40} (1)

     (b) Set B: {30, 33, 36, 39} (1)

     (c) Set C: {30, 35, 40} (1)

   (ii) (3)

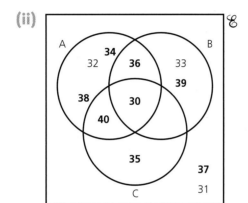

   (iii) $\frac{2}{11}$ (2)

10 (i) (a) (2)

	Soccer	Not soccer
Rugby	5	7
Not rugby	4	2

     (b) (2)

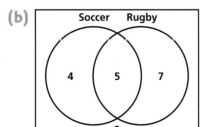

   (ii) (a) 5 boys (1)

     (b) 12 boys (1)

     (c) 9 boys (1)

   (iii) $\frac{2}{3}$ (2)